Simply Thoughtful

101 Ways for Adults to Honor Their Parents

by Leslie J. Barner

FAMILYLIFE

Bringing Timeless Principles Home

FamilyLife is a division of Campus Crusade for Christ, Inc., an evangelical Christian organization founded in 1951 by Bill Bright. FamilyLife was started in 1976 to help fulfill the Great Commission by strengthening marriages and families and then equipping them to go to the world with the gospel of Jesus Christ. Our FamilyLife Conferences are held in many cities throughout the United States. Information on all resources offered by FamilyLife may be obtained by either writing or calling us at the address and telephone numbers listed below.

Most Scriptures are quoted from the *New American Standard Bible.* Copyright © 1960, 1962, 1963, 1971, 1972, 1973, 1975, 1977 by the Lockman Foundation. Used by permission.

Other Scripture quotations are from:
The Holy Bible, New International Version (NIV) © 1973, 1978, 1984 by International Bible Society.
The Living Bible (TLB) © 1971. Used by permission of Tyndale House Publishers, Inc., Wheaton, IL 60187.

Simply Thoughtful
Copyright © 1998 by Leslie J. Barner
Published by FamilyLife

Designed by Lee Smith

Printed in the United States of America
ISBN 1-57229-109-5

FamilyLife
P.O. Box 8220
Little Rock, AR 72221-8220
(501) 223-8663
1-800-FL-TODAY
http://www.familylife-ccc.org

FAMILYLIFE™
Bringing Timeless Principles Home

All rights reserved. No part of this publication may be reproduced, stored in a retrieval system, or transmitted in any form or by any means—electronic, mechanical, photocopying, recording, or otherwise—without the prior written permission of the publisher.

Several years ago I received a letter from a young man asking what things I wish I had known when I was 20. If I could have gone back in time, I wished I had realized the importance of my parents in my life. I would have spent more time with Mom and Dad—telling them how much I loved and admired them.

It's tough to admit, but the first time I remember telling Mom and Dad, "I love you," was when I left for college as an 18-year old boy. The scene is forever etched in my mind. Boxes and suitcases stuffed the trunk and backseat of my white, four-door Chevy Bel-Air. As I prepared to leave home, I swallowed hard and fought back the tears. Then I said with a breaking voice, "Mom, Dad, I love you."

It was just ten short years later (after a wonderful visit with Mom and Dad), when the phone call came. It was my brother: Dad had died of a massive heart attack. I wondered if he really knew how much I loved him? Yes, for several years I had worked very hard to express my love to my parents. But my words seemed so hollow. Had I really honored Dad?

I pledged then that I would not wait until Mom died to let her know my feelings for her. And I have been true to my word—faithfully encouraging Mom and expressing my love through notes, calls, and visits. I crafted a written Tribute to her in 1984, carefully shaping phrases and special memories. I had it typeset and placed in a black wooden frame. It still hangs above the table where she eats her meals, as a reminder of my great love and appreciation for her.

Since you are reading *Simply Thoughtful,* you probably want to show your love and gratitude to your parents. Regardless of your circumstances or age, Leslie Barner has authored a book that will help you obey the fifth commandment and esteem your parents. *Simply Thoughtful* will jar your creativity and give you fresh new ways of showing your Mom and Dad how much they mean to you.

May God bless you mightily for honoring you parents. Believe me, you'll be glad you did!

Dennis Rainey
Executive Director
FamilyLife

God calls children of all ages to honor their parents. Doing so not only builds strong parent-child bonds, but also brings hope to strained relationships. Esteeming Mom and Dad is really a way of saying, "I love and appreciate you."

Simply Thoughtful has been written for adult children desiring to build and enhance their relationship with their parents. Although all ideas will not relate to your particular situation, they can be adapted easily and may even spark some of your own creative ideas.

We are told in Ephesians 6:2-3, "Honor your father and mother (which is the first commandment with a promise), that it may be well with you, and that you may live long on the earth." *Simply Thoughtful* is a wonderful tool that can help you actively follow this commandment. Pages are packed with fun, practical ideas, applying selected Scriptures to daily action points and everyday life. You may even want to memorize some of the Bible verses as a family.

You can recognize Mom and Dad in special ways by using this little book from time to time. By esteeming your parents—even when difficult—you will receive joy, experience God's promised blessings, and model obedience to this commandment for your own children.

Honoring your parents…what a legacy for generations to come!

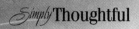

HONOR YOUR FATHER AND MOTHER
(which is the first commandment with a promise),
that it may be well with you, and that you may live
long on the earth.

Ephesians 6:2-3

1

Send a "thinking of you" card.

I thank my God in all my remembrance of you.

Philippians 1:3

2

Make videos for your parents of special times
in the lives of your children.

And do not neglect doing good and sharing; for with

such sacrifices God is pleased.

Hebrews 13:16

3

Ask them from time to time if there is anything special that you can do for them.

And if I have the gift of prophecy, and know all mysteries

and all knowledge; and if I have all faith, so as to remove

mountains, but do not have love, I am nothing.

1 Corinthians 13:2

4

Call just to ask, "How was your day?"

Give preference to one another in honor...

Romans 12:10b

5

Pray for them every day.

The effective prayer of a righteous man can accomplish much.

James 5:16b

6

Work hard at developing and/or maintaining a meaningful relationship with your parents.

Love...bears all things, believes all things, hopes all things, endures all things. Love never fails...

1 Corinthians 13:4-8

7

Make a special effort to call at least once a
week just to say, "I love you."

And may the Lord cause you to increase and abound in

love for one another...

1 Thessalonians 3:12

8

Remember their special days and acknowledge them.

(Hint: If you cannot be present at their celebration, let them
know you care through a phone call, gift, or card.)

This is the day which the Lord has made; Let us

rejoice and be glad in it.

Psalm 118:24

9

Take your parents out for dinner and enjoy some special time together.

For it is God who is at work in you, both to will

and to work for His good pleasure.

Philippians 2:13

10

Choose your words carefully when you differ with them.

A gentle answer turns away wrath, but a harsh word

stirs up anger.

Proverbs 15:1

11

When there is a disagreement, watch your temper and try to remain calm. Don't say or do things you may later regret.

But the fruit of the Spirit is...self-control...

Galatians 5:22-23

12

Bless them by spending a day cleaning an area of their home.
(Hint: Maybe the windows need washing.)

I can do all things through Him who strengthens me.

Philippians 4:13

13

Send an "encouragement" card when you know they need some kind words.

Therefore encourage one another, and build up one another...

1 Thessalonians 5:11

14

Share Jesus with them, if they do not already know Him.

[Jesus said,]..."Go home to your people and report to them what great things the Lord has done for you, and how He had mercy on you."

Mark 5:19

15

Make sure your parents have transportation to
and from church each Sunday.
(Hint: If they need transportation, and you do not live nearby,
enlist the help of a relative, friend, or church member.)

...let us not love with word or with tongue, but in deed

and truth.

1 John 3:18

16

Offer to do the grocery shopping for them now and then.

(Hint: They can provide the shopping list and the grocery money—unless you are financially able to bless in this way.)

...through love serve one another.

Galatians 5:13

17

Send them to a Christian retreat for physical refreshment and spiritual renewal.

He who refreshes others will himself be refreshed.

Proverbs 11:25b (New International Version)

18

Send them postcards when you are on a trip
with your family.

Even so, every good tree bears good fruit...

Matthew 7:17

19

Relate to your parents openly and honestly.

The integrity of the upright will guide them...

Proverbs 11:3

20

Buy a good book for them on a topic they enjoy.
(Hint: Have it gift-wrapped and sent to them.)

And the Lord will repay each man for his

righteousness and his faithfulness...

1 Samuel 26:23

21

Occasionally leave uplifting messages on their answering machine.

(Hint: You could leave a "thought for the day" from your favorite devotional, or an "I'm thinking of you" message.)

A soothing tongue is a tree of life...

Proverbs 15:4

22

If you have the necessary skills, offer to repair
their car (or take it to an auto repair shop).

The generous man will be prosperous...

Proverbs 11:25

23

Be understanding and forgiving when they make mistakes.

And be kind to one another, tender-hearted, forgiving each other, just as God in Christ also has forgiven you.

Ephesians 4:32

24

Compliment them often.

(Hint: You can comment positively about their appearance, a
dress, tie, hairstyle, or on how well they do something.)

Continue to love each other with true brotherly love.

Hebrews 13:1 (TLB)

25

Do not speak ill of your parents to others.

Let the words of my mouth and the meditation of my heart be acceptable in Thy sight, O Lord, my rock and my Redeemer.

Psalm 19:14

Simply **Thoughtful**

26

Get them a subscription to a magazine you
think they would enjoy.

But the fruit of the Spirit is...kindness...

Galatians 5:22

27

While you're visiting them one evening, leave a loving note on their pillow (so they'll see it when they go to bed).

...love one another, even as I have loved you...

John 13:34

28

Write a list of why you think they are special,
and mail it to them.

Pleasant words are a honeycomb, sweet to the soul and

healing to the bones.

Proverbs 16:24

29

Plan a special family dinner for them at which they are the "guests of honor."

Render to all what is due them...honor to whom honor.

Romans 13:7

30

Work hard to get along well with your parents
and all other family members.

If possible, so far as it depends on you, be at peace

with all men.

Romans 12:18

31

When they are not feeling well, help out as
much as you can by being there for them.
(Hint: Make tea or soup, run errands, drive them to the doctor's
office, or read to them at their bedside. If you live far away, call
often to check on them, and send them a get-well card.)

...if we love one another, God abides in us, and His

love is perfected in us.

1 John 4:12

32

Give them a hug when you see them.

...fervently love one another from the heart.

1 Peter 1:22

33

Be a good listener when they want to talk.

And just as you want people to treat you, treat them in the same way.

Luke 6:31

34

Be caring when they are experiencing
tough times.

Therefore my beloved brethren, be steadfast, immovable,

always abounding in the work of the Lord, knowing that

your toil is not in vain in the Lord.

1 Corinthians 15:58

35

Let them know when you are going through tough times.

Bear one another's burdens, and thus fulfill the law

of Christ.

Galatians 6:2

36

Mail them a gift certificate from a restaurant
or beauty salon, or for a round of golf, etc.

In response to all he [Jesus] has done for us, let us

outdo each other in being helpful and kind to each other

and in doing good.

Hebrews 10:24 (TLB)

37

Send them a special hand-written letter thanking them for their love, support, and patience through your teen years.

Do not withhold good from those to whom it is due,

when it is in your power to do it.

Proverbs 3:27

38

Be patient when you feel they are nagging.

A man's discretion makes him slow to anger, and it is

his glory to overlook a transgression.

Proverbs 19:11

39

Give Mom a break by cooking dinner for your parents at their home one evening.

But in everything commending ourselves as servants

of God...

2 Corinthians 6:4

40

Honor your parents by naming one of your children after them.

(Even if you use one of their names for your child's middle name, it would bring them unspeakable joy and create a special bond with their grandchild.)

A good name is to be more desired than great riches...

Proverbs 22:1

41

If you think they are meddling, express this to them in a gentle, loving way.

...reprove, rebuke, exhort, with great patience and instruction.

2 Timothy 4:2

42

Send them a bouquet of flowers or a plant this week to say "I love you."

Let your gentleness be evident to all. The Lord is near.

Philippians 4:5 (NIV)

43

Share your good news and accomplishments
with them.

But the fruit of the Spirit is...joy...

Galatians 5:22

44

Rejoice in their good news and accomplishments.

Rejoice with those who rejoice...

Romans 12:15

45

Take a portrait with your brothers and sisters and give it to your parents on a special occasion.

(A portrait of their adult children together would bless them abundantly.)

Behold, children are a gift of the Lord...

Psalm 127:3

46

Invite them to go on a vacation with you.

And do not neglect doing good and sharing; for with such sacrifices God is pleased.

Hebrews 13:16

47

Take the time to encourage them when they are feeling down.

(Hint: You could call, visit, or send them a card.)

Anxiety in the heart of a man weighs it down, but a good word makes it glad.

Proverbs 12:25

48

Remember to say you're sorry when you are wrong, and ask for their forgiveness.

...clothe yourselves with humility toward one another, for God

is opposed to the proud, but gives grace to the humble.

1 Peter 5:5

49

Ask your mom or dad to help you with a
project where they have particular expertise.
(Hint: If your mom sews, have her help you make those new
drapes. If your dad is a handyman, ask for his advice regarding
some home repairs that have been on the back burner.)

...that their hearts may be encouraged, having been knit

together in love...

Colossians 2:2

50

Respect their decisions—even if you do not agree with them.

...for you will be doing what is good and right in the

sight of the Lord your God.

Deuteronomy 12:28

51

Be supportive when they decide to make a
life-change (large or small).

...always seek after that which is good for one another...

1 Thessalonians 5:15b

52

Write them a special "thank you for everything" letter that they can cherish.

Say only what is good and helpful to those you are

talking to, and what will give them a blessing.

Ephesians 4:29b (TLB)

53

Send them a tape-recorded message of a
favorite devotional or special sermon.

*In everything you do, put God first, and he will direct
you and crown your efforts with success.*

Proverbs 3:6 (TLB)

54

Share your goals and dreams with them.

Where there is no guidance the people fall...

Proverbs 11:14

55

Let them know your prayer requests.

The effective prayer of a righteous man can accomplish much.

James 5:16b

56

Tell your parents how God has answered
your prayers.

Then our mouth was filled with laughter, and our

tongue with joyful shouting; then they said among the

nations, "The Lord has done great things for them."

Psalm 126:2

57

Keep your promises.

God delights in those who keep their promises...

Proverbs 12:22 (TLB)

58

Take an interest in their jobs, hobbies, and how they spend their time.

(Hint: Ask how things are going. Accompany them on a fishing trip, to the golf course, or to a concert of their favorite artist.)

Do not merely look out for your own personal interests, but also for the interests of others.

Philippians 2:4

59

Dwell on the good things about your parents.

...Fix your thoughts on what is...pure and lovely, and

dwell on the fine good things in others...

Philippians 4:8 (TLB)

60

Model for your children the biblical principles,
values, character traits, and good manners
you learned from your parents.

*Remember those who led you, who spoke the word of
God to you; and considering the result of their conduct,
imitate their faith.*

Hebrews 13:7

61

Make sure you allow your parents to play an
important role in your children's lives.

...for whatever a man sows, this he will also reap.

Galatians 6:7

62

Send them a letter or card honoring their accomplishments or unique character traits.

I have great confidence in you: I take great pride in you...

2 Corinthians 7:4 (NIV)

63

Respect their privacy.

Therefore, however you want people to treat you, so treat them...

Matthew 7:12

Simply **Thoughtful**

64

When there is conflict, deal with your anger in love. Seek to bring about resolution and reconciliation.

Be angry, and yet do not sin; do not let the sun go

down on your anger...

Ephesians 4:26

65

Surprise them with a car wash.

But the greatest among you shall be your servant.

Matthew 23:11

66

Send them a tape-recorded message of love
and appreciation from you or your children.

...how delightful is a timely word!

Proverbs 15:23

67

As much as possible, include them in the
family traditions you are forming with
your children.

By this all men will know that you are My

disciples, if you have love for one another.

John 13:35

68

Plan a movie night for them at your home (or theirs, if they prefer).

(Hint: Rent some of their favorite videos, and don't forget the popcorn!)

Be hospitable to one another...

1 Peter 4:9

69

When your parents invite you over for dinner, pick up their favorite dessert on the way and surprise them!

Your own soul is nourished when you are kind...

Proverbs 11:17 (TLB)

70

Have a portrait of your family made for them.

(Hint: Select a beautiful frame for the portrait that would compliment the decor of your parents' home.)

...put on a heart of compassion, kindness...

Colossians 3:12

71

Show that you value the things that they feel
are important.

...but with humility of mind let each of you regard one

another as more important than himself.

Philippians 2:3

72

If at all possible, make yourself available to them when they need you.

And let us not lose heart in doing good, for in due

time we shall reap if we do not grow weary.

Galatians 6:9

73

Plan a "Fix-It Day" to do some of their needed household repairs.

Whatever your hand finds to do, verily, do it with all

your might...

Ecclesiastes 9:10

Simply **Thoughtful**

74

If your parents are in financial need, help
them if you have the means to do so.
(Hint: You could arrange to regularly pay one of their utility bills
if they are experiencing a monthly income shortage.)

Commit your works to the Lord...

Proverbs 16:3

75

Always try to maintain a good attitude, even when things are not going as well as you would like in your relationship with them.

Be completely humble and gentle, be patient, bearing with one another in love. Make every effort to keep the unity of the Spirit through the bond of peace.

Ephesians 4:2-3 (NIV)

*Simply*Thoughtful

76

Send your parents the registration fee for that
water aerobics class or golf lesson they've
been talking about taking.

Make the most of every opportunity you have for

doing good.

Ephesians 5:16 (TLB)

77

Take the initiative to communicate with your parents and deal with tough issues.

Above all, love each other deeply, because love covers over a multitude of sins.

1 Peter 4:8 (NIV)

78

Ask their opinions and advice.

A wise man will hear and increase in learning, and a

man of understanding will acquire wise counsel.

Proverbs 1:5

79

Surprise them by mowing their lawn.

Whatever you do, do your work heartily, as for the Lord rather than for men...

Colossians 3:23

80

Send a balloon bouquet this week with "You are special" as the central theme.

But the fruit of the Spirit is...goodness...

Galatians 5:22

81

When they ask you to do something within
your abilities, do it without complaining.

Do all things without grumbling or disputing...

Philippians 2:14

82

Call one morning to read them a passage of Scripture and an inspirational thought for the day.

Thy word is a lamp to my feet, and a light to my path.

Psalm 119:105

83

Keep yourself from bringing up past issues to
retaliate for former hurts.

...But one thing I do: forgetting what is behind and straining

toward what is ahead, I press on toward the goal to win the prize

for which God has called me heavenward in Christ Jesus.

Philippians 3:13 (NIV)

84

Surprise them on their birthdays with a special delivery package.

(Hint: Include a tape recording of your family singing "Happy Birthday." You could also include some other loving messages on the tape.)

...fervently love one another from the heart.

1 Peter 1:22

85

Cherish the time you have together—make the most of it!

So teach us to number our days, that we may present to Thee a heart of wisdom.

Psalm 90:12

Simply **Thoughtful**

86

On Valentine's Day, send your parents a special
gift, balloon bouquet, or flowers. You may
want to include a card saying, "I love you."

...but the greatest of these is love.

1 Corinthians 13:13

87

Don't hold grudges against them. Forgive past mistakes. Remember, life is short.

(Hint: Talk to your parents about past hurts in a non-threatening way. Let them know you forgive them and appreciate them for the things they did right. Then, release them from past offenses.)

Be gentle and ready to forgive; never hold grudges.

Remember, the Lord forgave you, so you must forgive others.

Colossians 3:13 (TLB)

88

Hold them accountable for their health—remind
them to get check-ups, observe diets, etc.

Be devoted to one another in brotherly love; give

preference to one another in honor...

Romans 12:10

89

Comfort them when they have lost a friend or received bad news.

And so, as those who have been chosen of God, holy and beloved, put on a heart of compassion, kindness, humility, gentleness and patience.

Colossians 3:12

90

Offer to paint their house, if needed.

So then, while we have opportunity, let us do good to

all men...

Galatians 6:10

91

Get their favorite Scripture engraved on a plaque for them to display in their home.

The law of the Lord is perfect, restoring the soul; the testimony of the Lord is sure, making wise the simple. The precepts of the Lord are right, rejoicing the heart...

Psalm 19:7-8

92

Share childhood stories with your family that capture the love and fun that you had growing up with your parents.

...whatever you do, do all to the glory of God.

1 Corinthians 10:31

93

When they say "No" to something you think would be good for them to do, or feel that they cannot do a certain thing (that may be good for them to do), encourage them, but don't try to force them to change their minds.

...Love does not demand its own way...

1 Corinthians 13:5 (TLB)

94

Write them a letter of appreciation for everything they taught you.

(Hint: Talk about the values they taught you, and thank them for all the times they said "No." Tell them how you've benefited over the years from their discipline, and how it has helped you in your own parenting.)

I have directed you in the way of wisdom; I have led you in upright paths.

Proverbs 4:11

95

As a Christian, always let your light shine
when you're with your parents.

Let your light shine before men in such a way that they

may see your good works, and glorify your Father who

is in heaven.

Matthew 5:16

96

On your birthday, pick up a little gift for your mom and dad, and a card to say, "Thank you for being God's instrument to give me life."

...and remember the words of the Lord Jesus, that He Himself said, "It is more blessed to give than to receive."

Acts 20:35

97

If they are aware you have a need and they offer to help, allow them the opportunity— don't let pride get in the way.

A man's pride will bring him low, but a humble spirit

will obtain honor.

Proverbs 29:23

Simply **Thoughtful**

98

Next time you visit, take out the family photo albums and go down memory lane with them.
(Hint: You may even want to play some "Oldies but Goodies" to enhance the mood.)

Commit to the Lord whatever you do, and your plans will succeed.

Proverbs 16:3 (NIV)

99

Send them a copy of a meaningful poem or
quote that will make them smile.

A joyful heart is good medicine...

Proverbs 17:22

Simply **Thoughtful**

100

The next time you visit your parents on an overnight trip, get up extra early to serve them breakfast in bed.

...but through love serve one another.

Galatians 5:13

101

Give God thanks for your parents always!

Rejoice always...in everything give thanks; for this is God's will for you in Christ Jesus.

1 Thessalonians 5:16-18

Simply **Thoughtful**

My Idea

_____

_____

_____

Scripture:

_____

_____

My Idea

_____

_____

_____

Scripture:

_____

_____

*Simply*Thoughtful

My Idea

_____

_____

_____

Scripture:

_____

_____

About the Author

Leslie Barner is a wife, mother, and writer for FamilyLife, a division of Campus Crusade for Christ. She is the author of *Blessings and Blunders on Baxter Street—Lessons on Virtue* (for children), *Xtreme Choices for Excellent Living* (for teens), and *Our Legacy of Love* (for couples). She is also the editor of *Simply Romantic Ideas for Husbands* and *Simply Romantic Ideas for Wives.* Leslie and her husband, Aubrey, reside in Little Rock, Arkansas, with their four daughters, Desiree, Tiffany, Brittany, and Krystina.

W hether you are 15 or 50 years old, God wants you to honor your mother and father. Through the pages of *The Tribute and the Promise,* Dennis Rainey tells how you can build a relationship with your parents that will glorify God and bring a blessing to your own life. Heartwarming stories and practical suggestions make this a book that can change your life.

Call **1-800-FL-TODAY** or visit our Web site at **www.familylife-ccc.org** to order this and other FamilyLife resources.

Product #1062   Retails for $12.95

FAMILYLIFE™
Bringing Timeless Principles Home